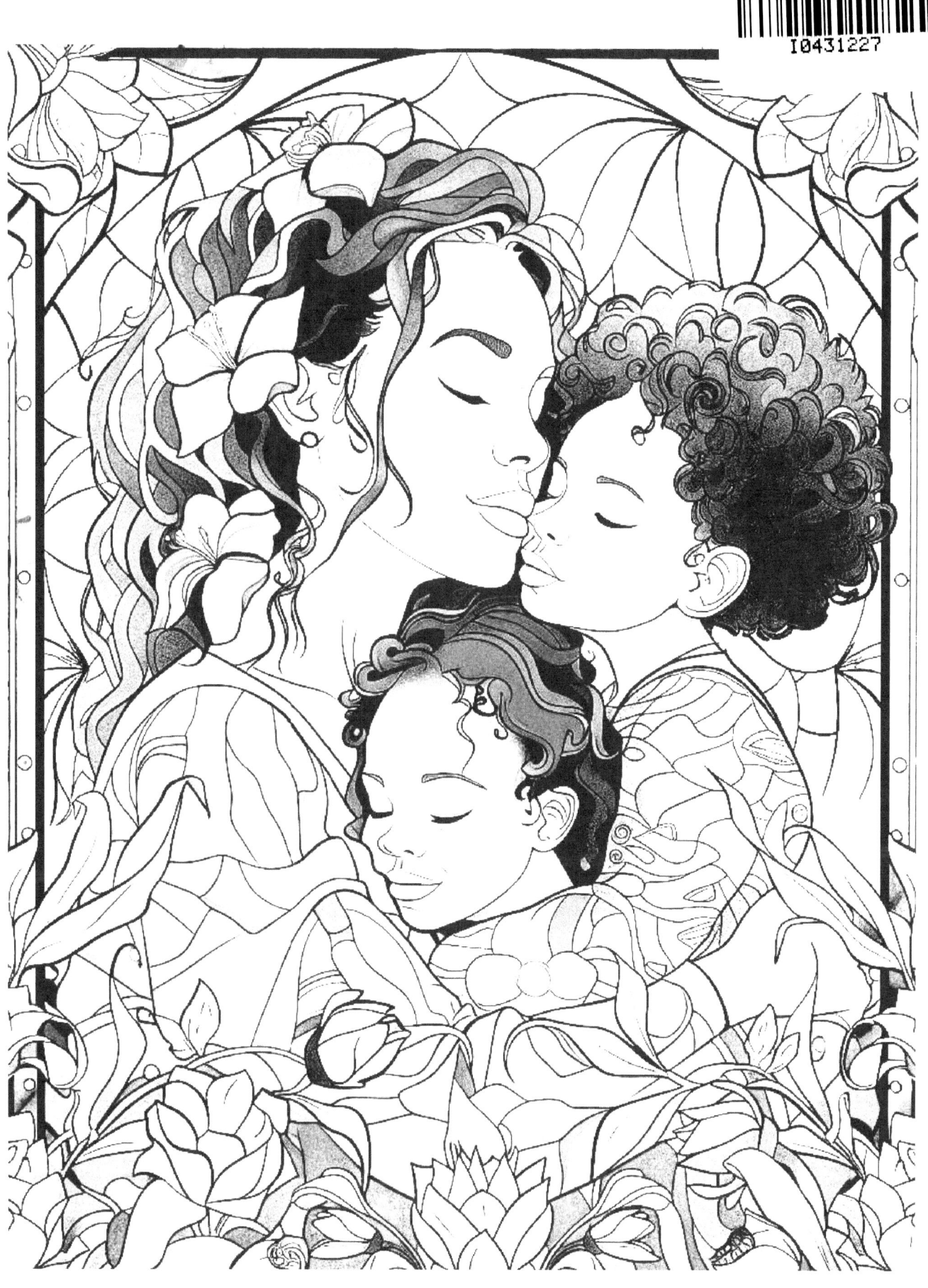

Copyright 2024

All rights reserved.

No portion of this book may be reproduced in any form without written permission from the publisher or author, except as permitted by U.S. copyright law.

WELCOME THE TO
EMBRACE MOTHER'S COLORING BOOK
AND QUOTE'S

"Discover endless grace in a mother's love and the wisdom to face the world with open hearts and resilient spirits through her teachings. Embrace gratitude for Mom, for in her strength, we find our own. In her love, we discover endless grace and, in her teachings, the wisdom to face the world with open hearts and resilience."

<u>Anita Persaud</u>

EMBRACE MOTHER'S QUOTE'S

A mother's embrace: where the palette of life finds its most beautiful expression."

"In the art of motherhood, every hug and kiss paint the masterpiece of a child's heart."

"Motherhood—where the simplest moments become the most vibrant memories, colored with love."

"Through a mother's love, we learn that life's most beautiful colors are felt, not just seen."

"A mother's embrace is the canvas where the first strokes of life's painting begin, filled with the colors of love and guidance."

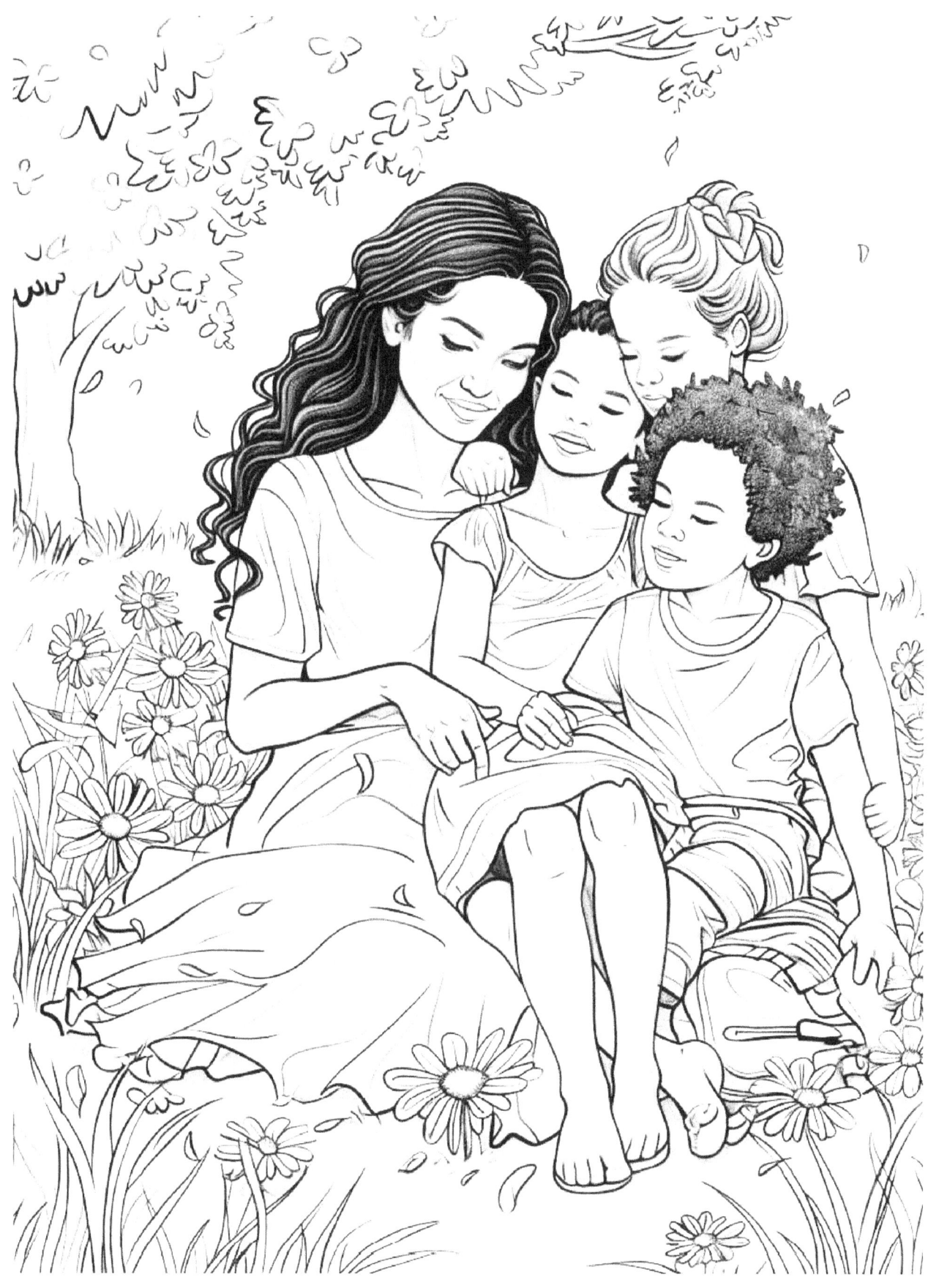

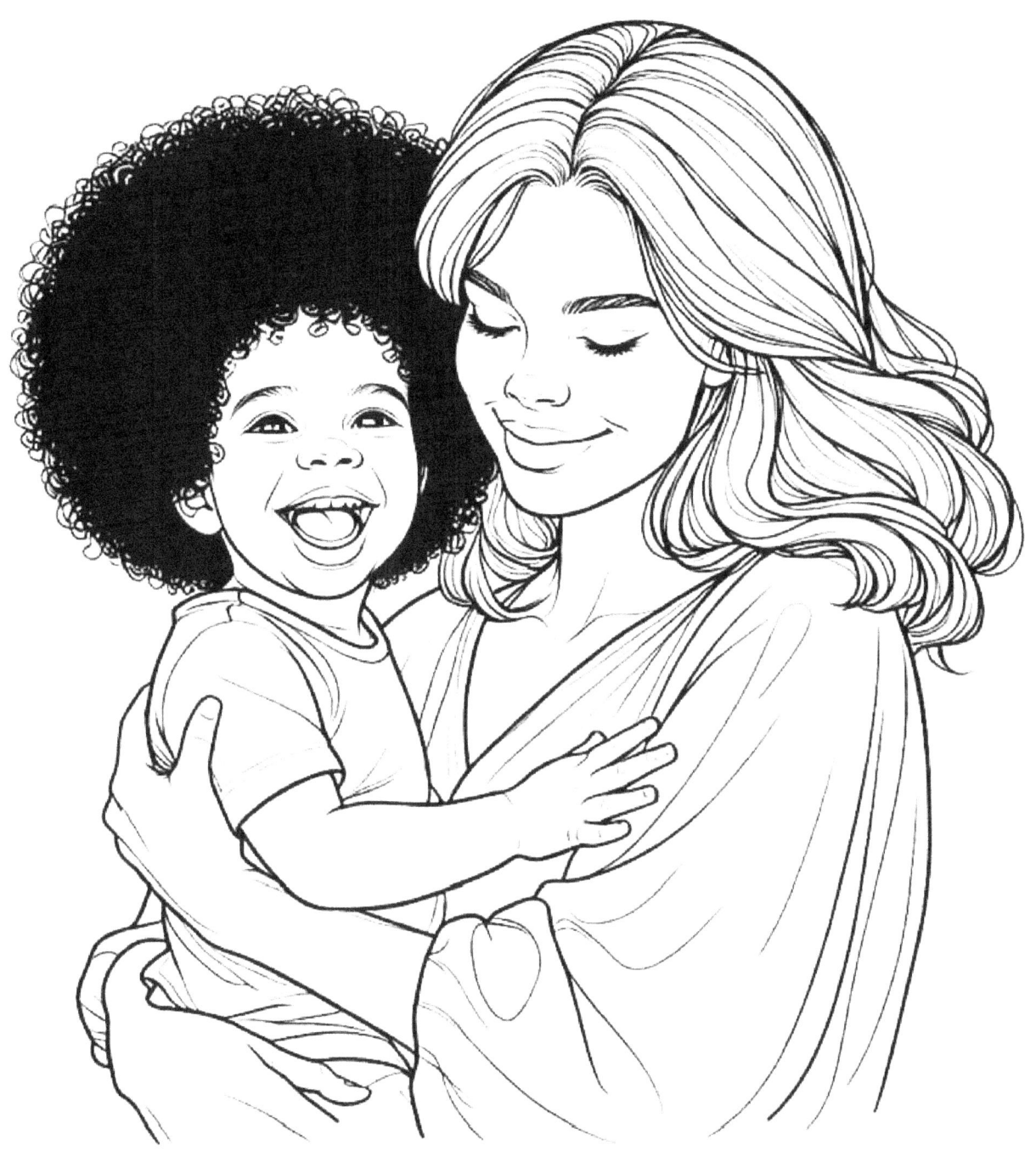

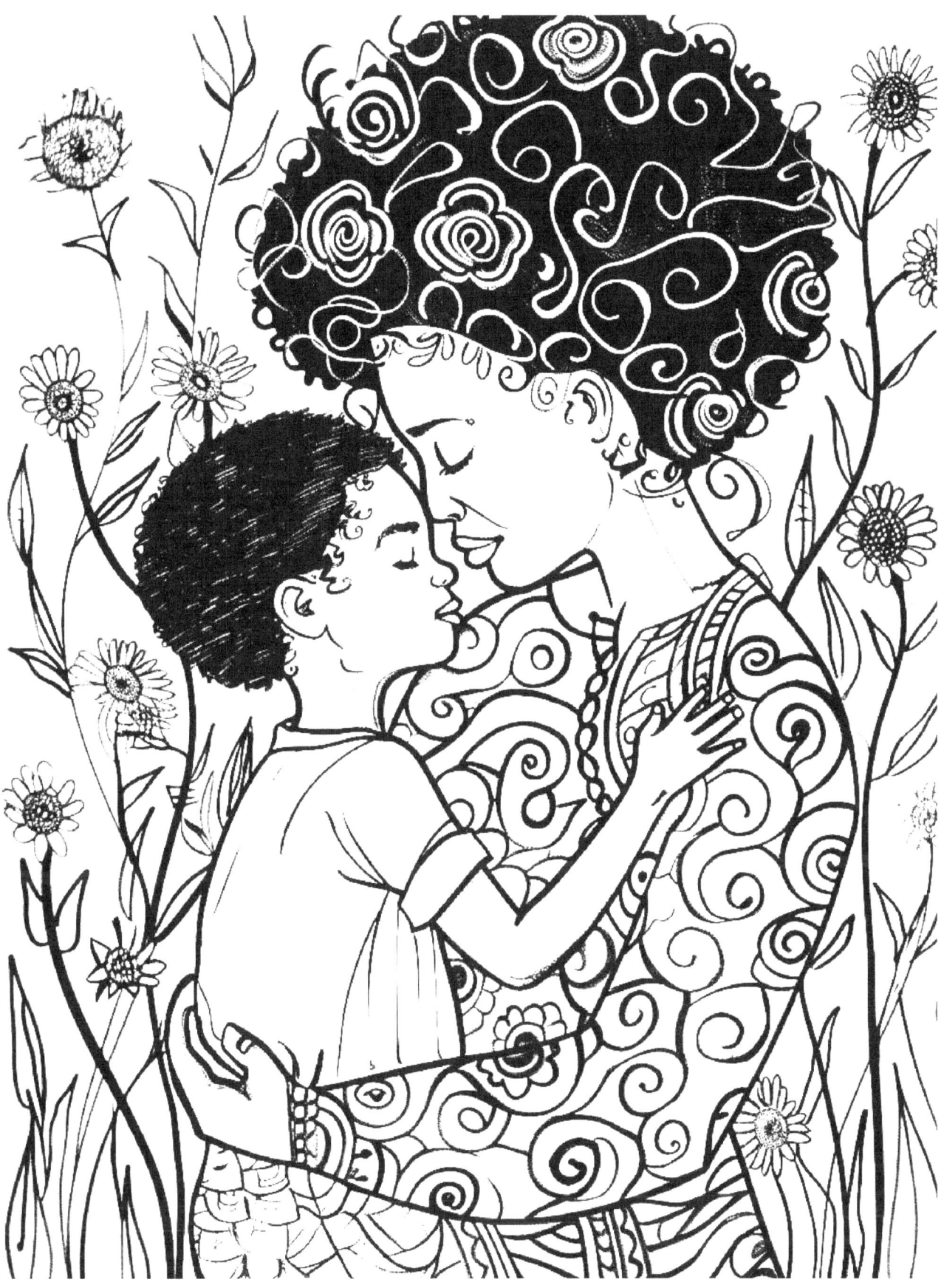

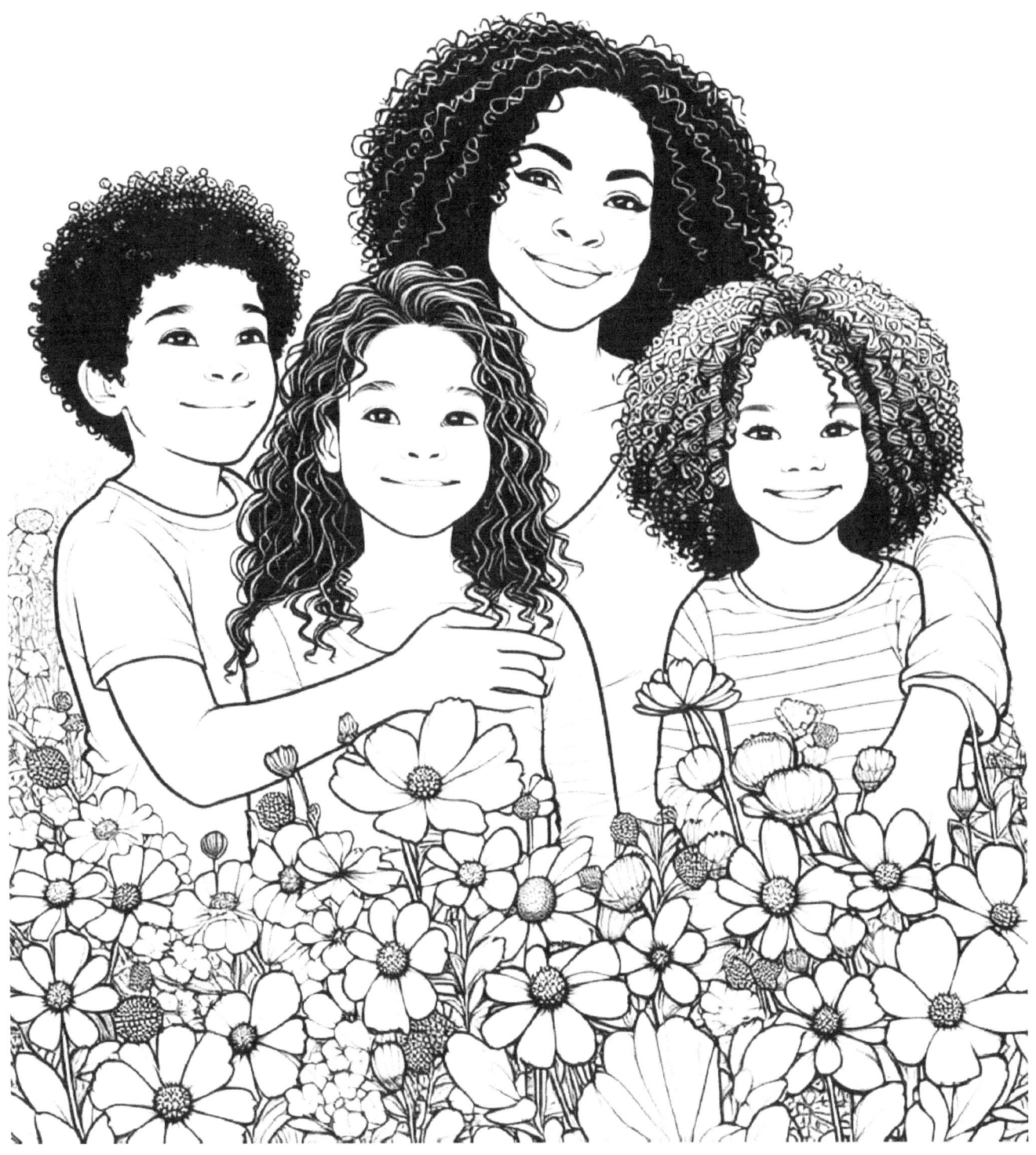

Copyright 2024

All rights reserved.

No portion of this book may be reproduced in any form without written permission from the publisher or author, except as permitted by U.S. copyright law.

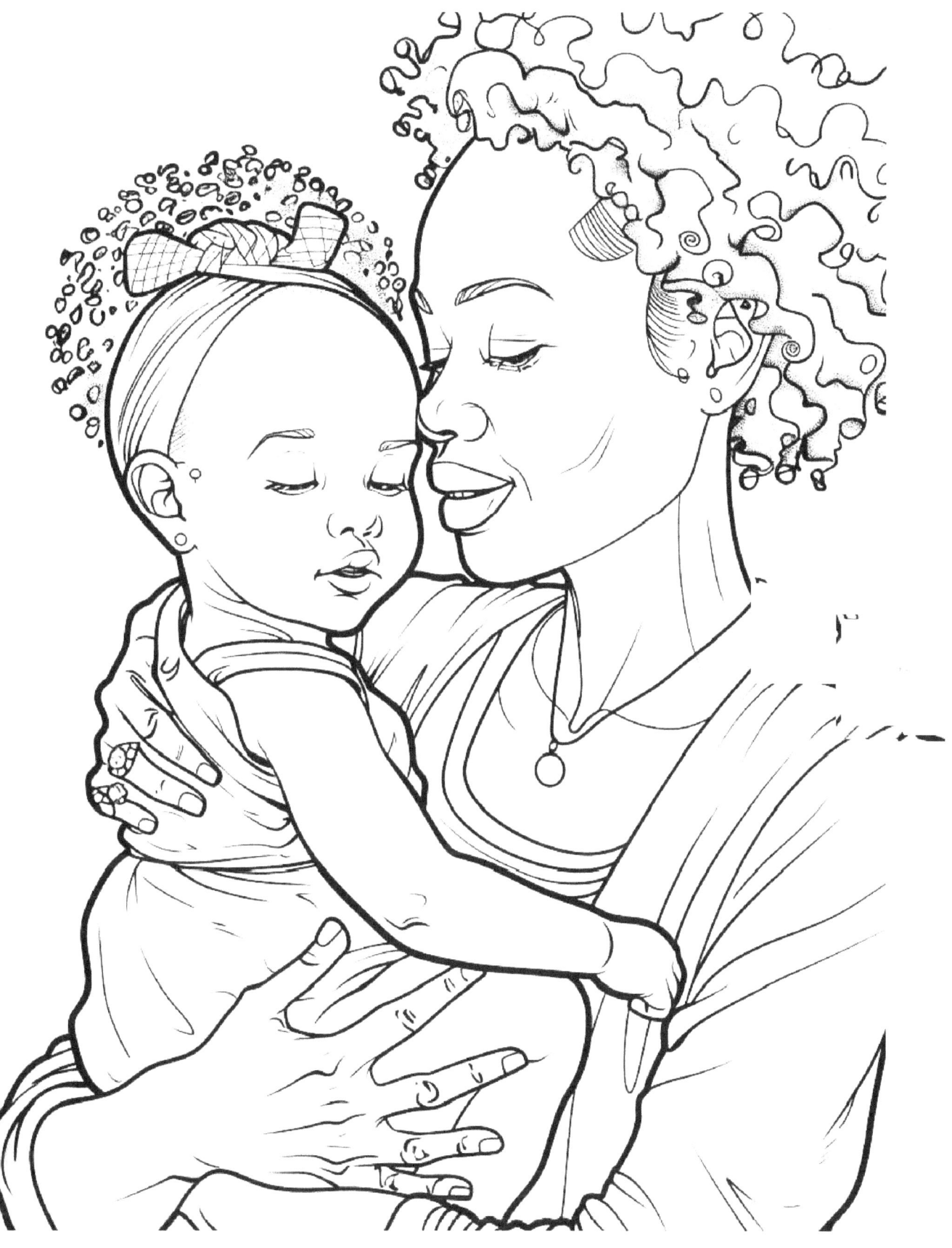

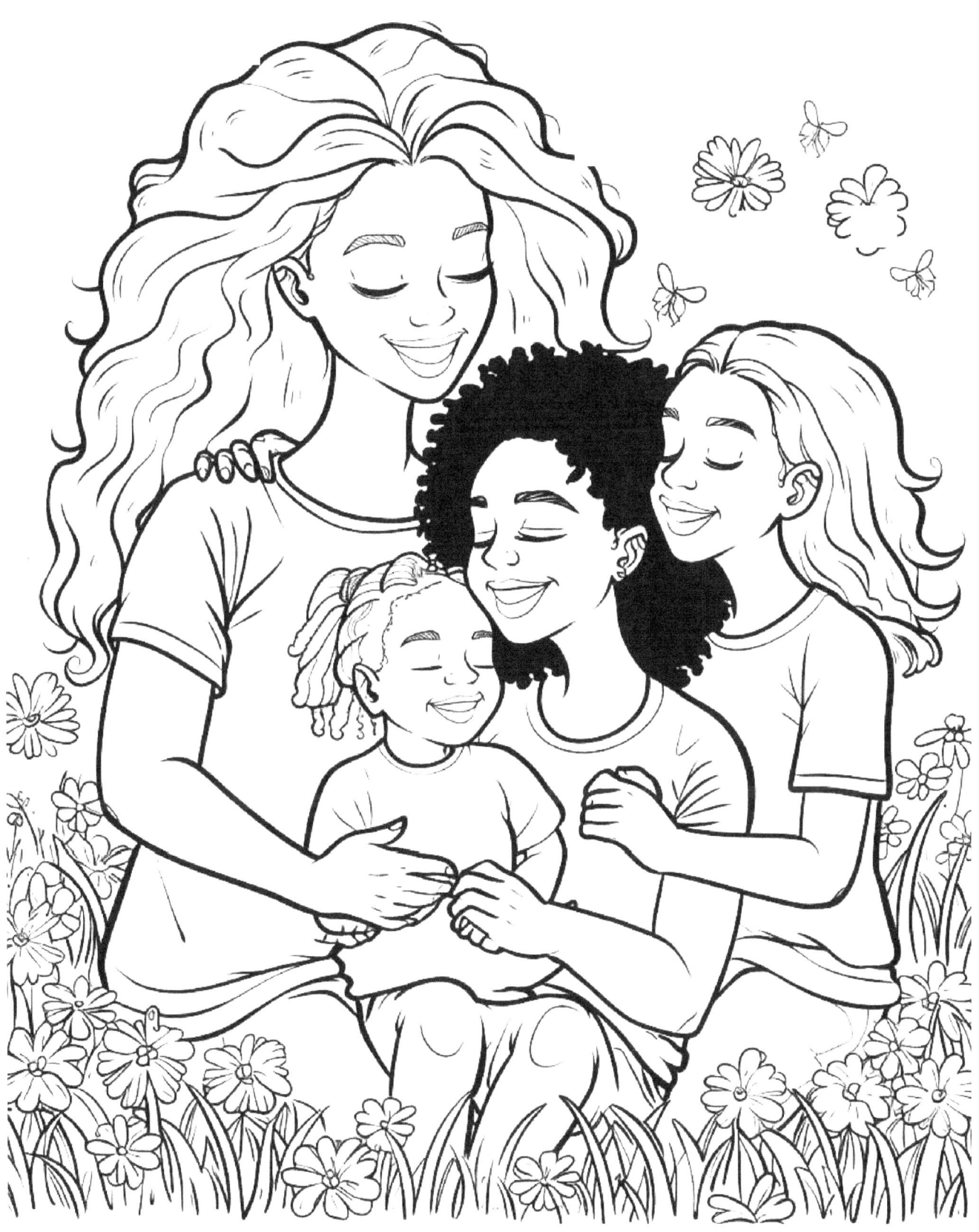

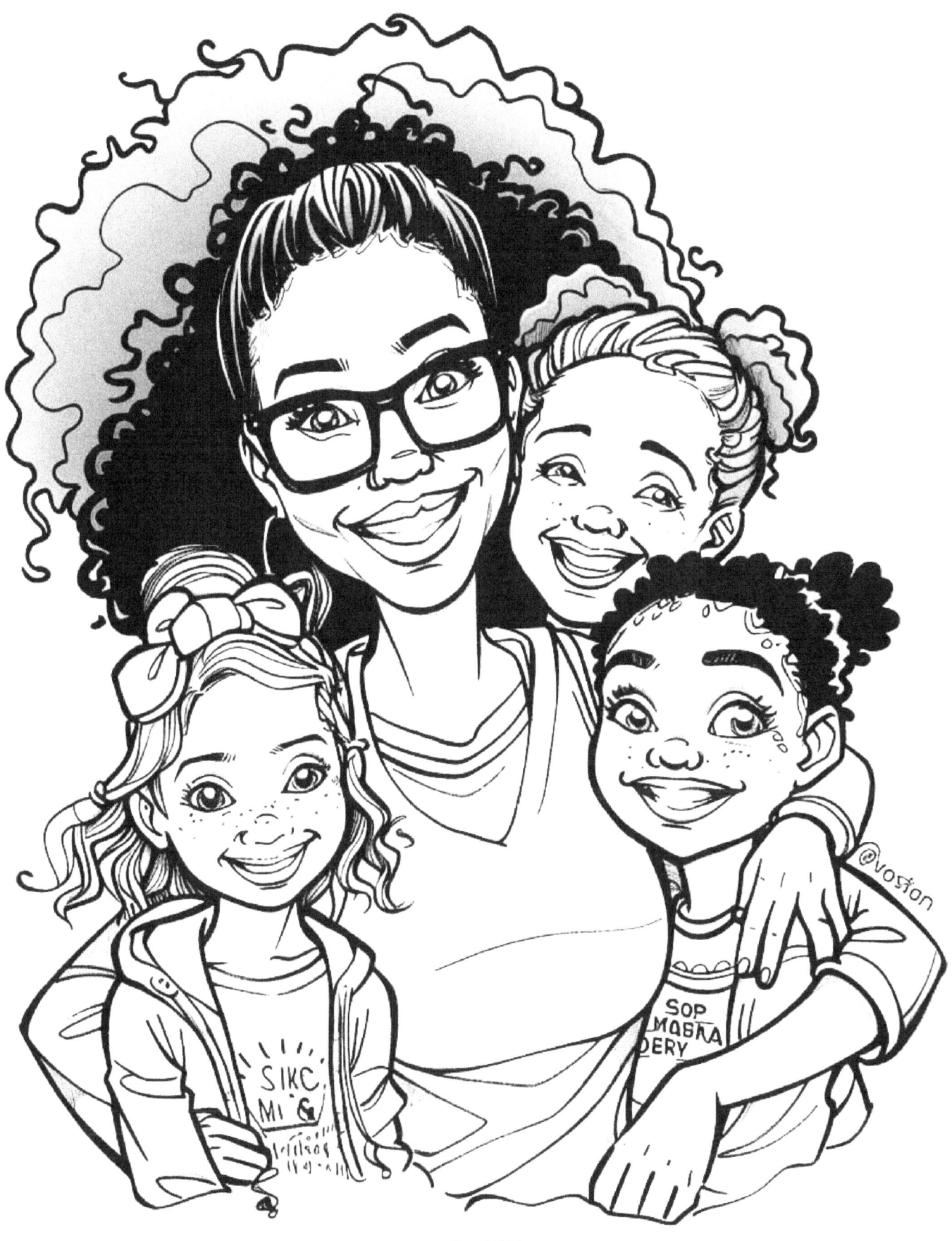

Copyright 2024
All rights reserved.

No portion of this book may be reproduced in any form without written permission from the publisher or author, except as permitted by U.S. copyright law.

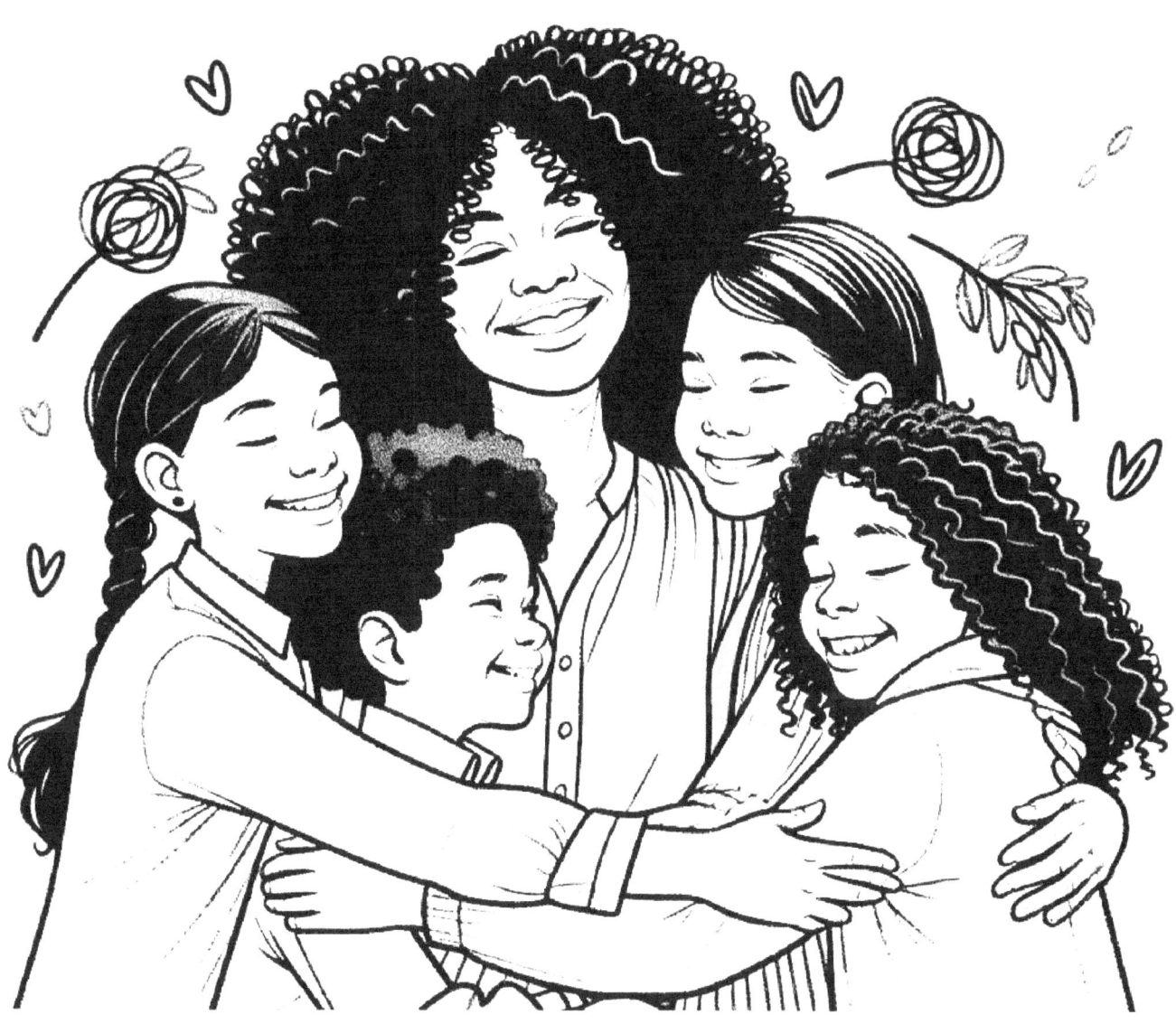

Copyright 2024

All rights reserved.

No portion of this book may be reproduced in any form without written permission from the publisher or author, except as permitted by U.S. copyright law.

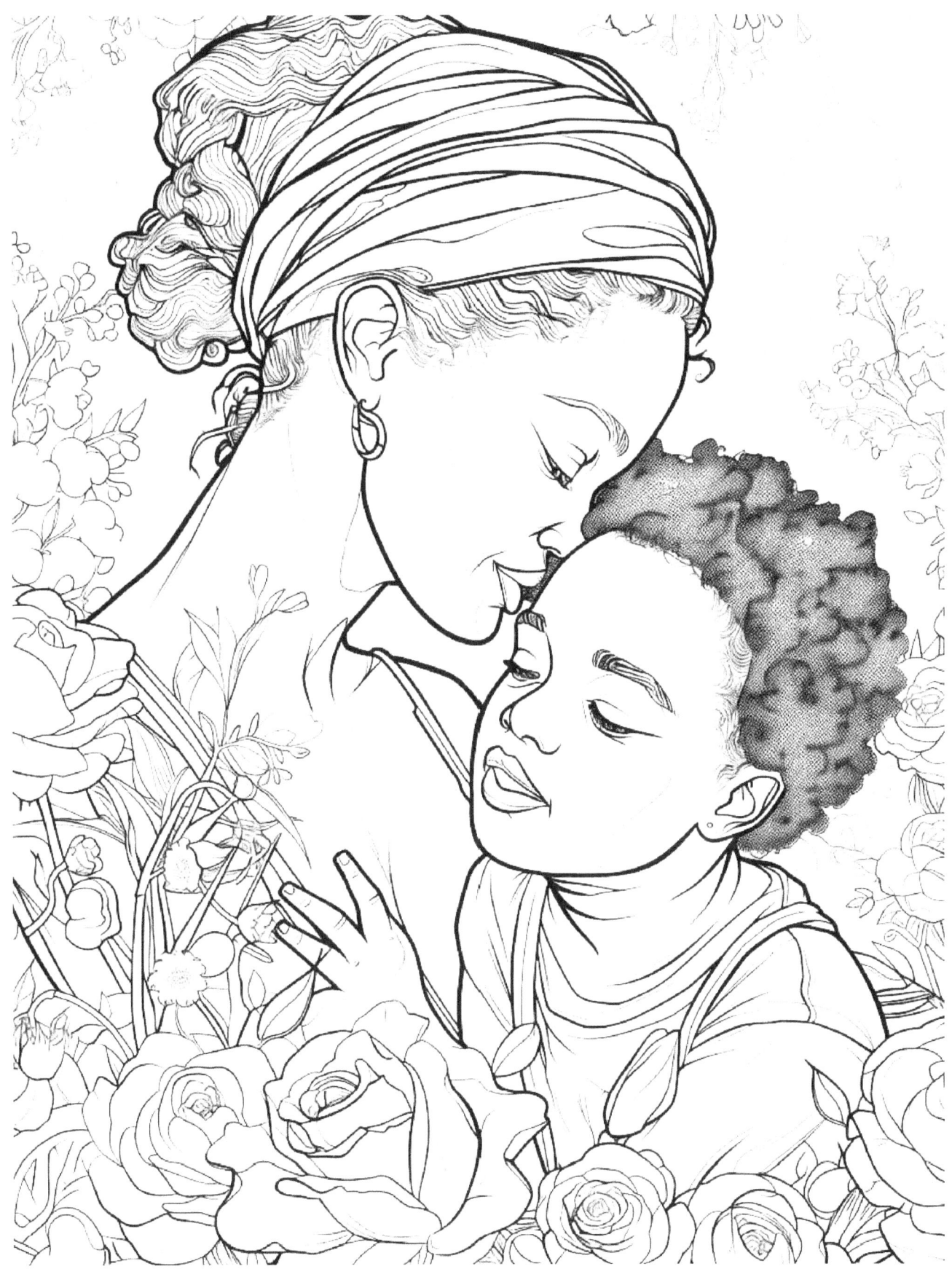

Copyright 2024

All rights reserved.

No portion of this book may be reproduced in any form without written permission from the publisher or author, except as permitted by U.S. copyright law.

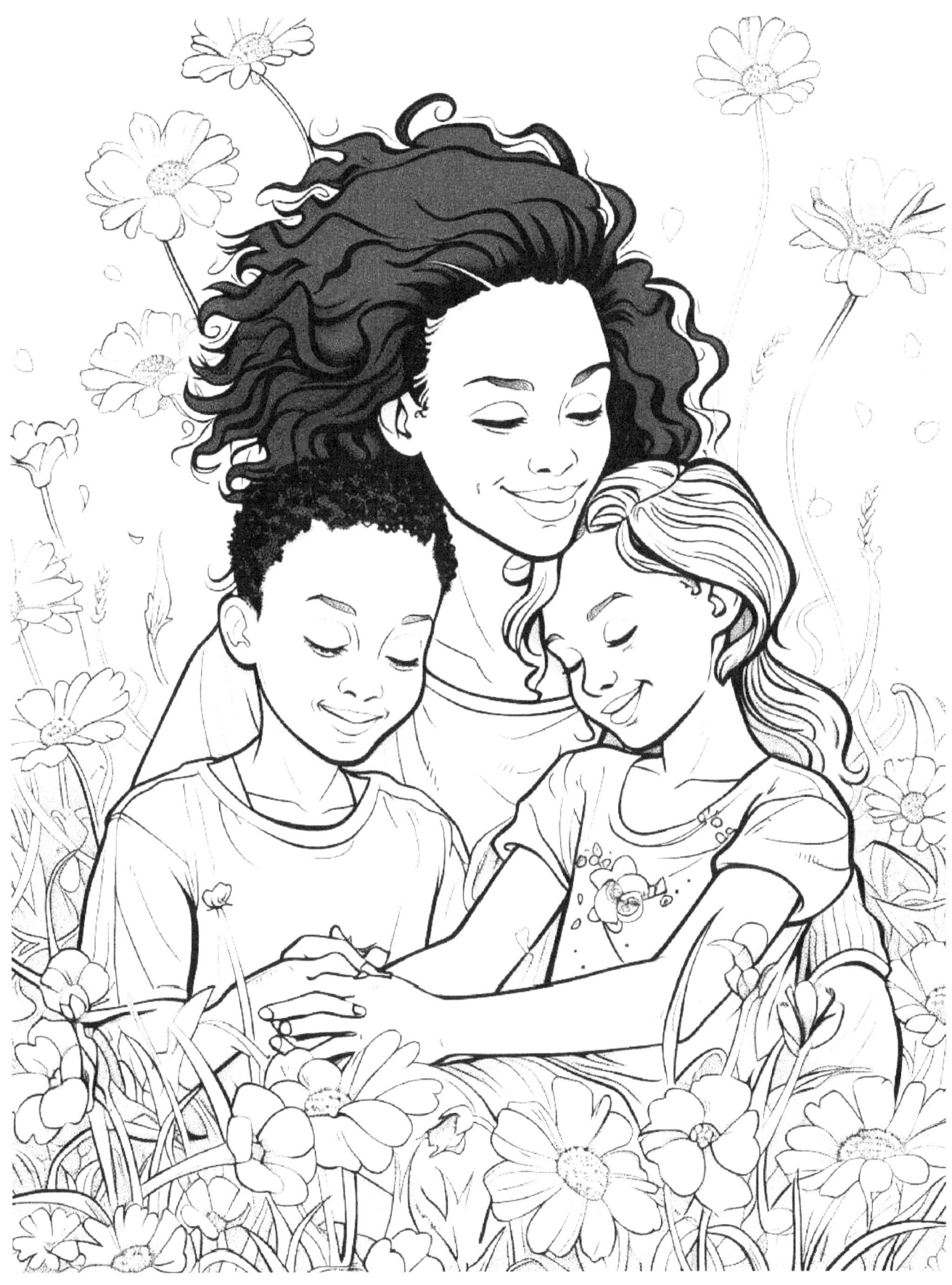

Copyright 2024

All rights reserved.

No portion of this book may be reproduced in any form without written permission from the publisher or author, except as permitted by U.S. copyright law.

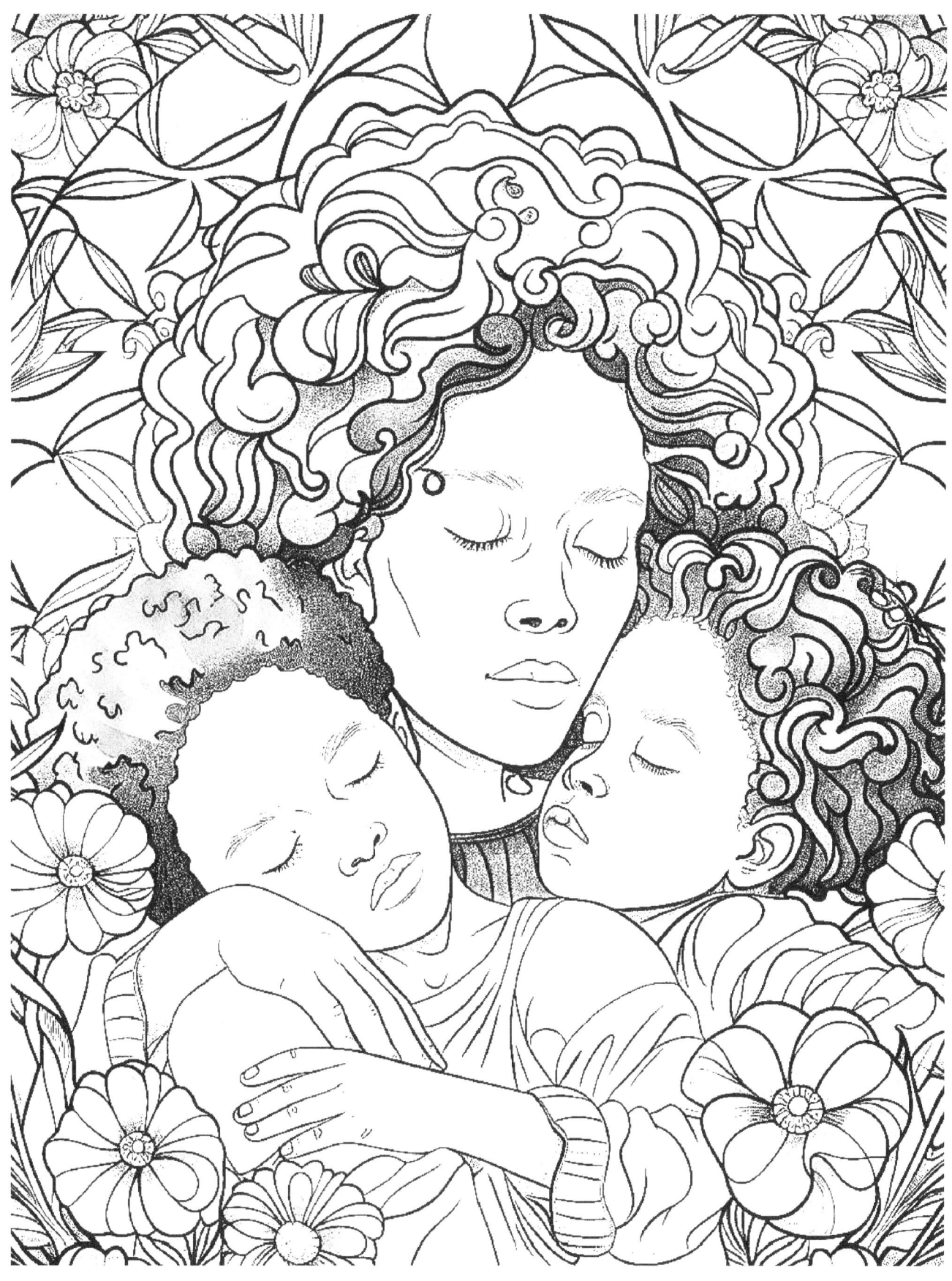

Copyright 2024

All rights reserved.

No portion of this book may be reproduced in any form without written permission from the publisher or author, except as permitted by U.S. copyright law.

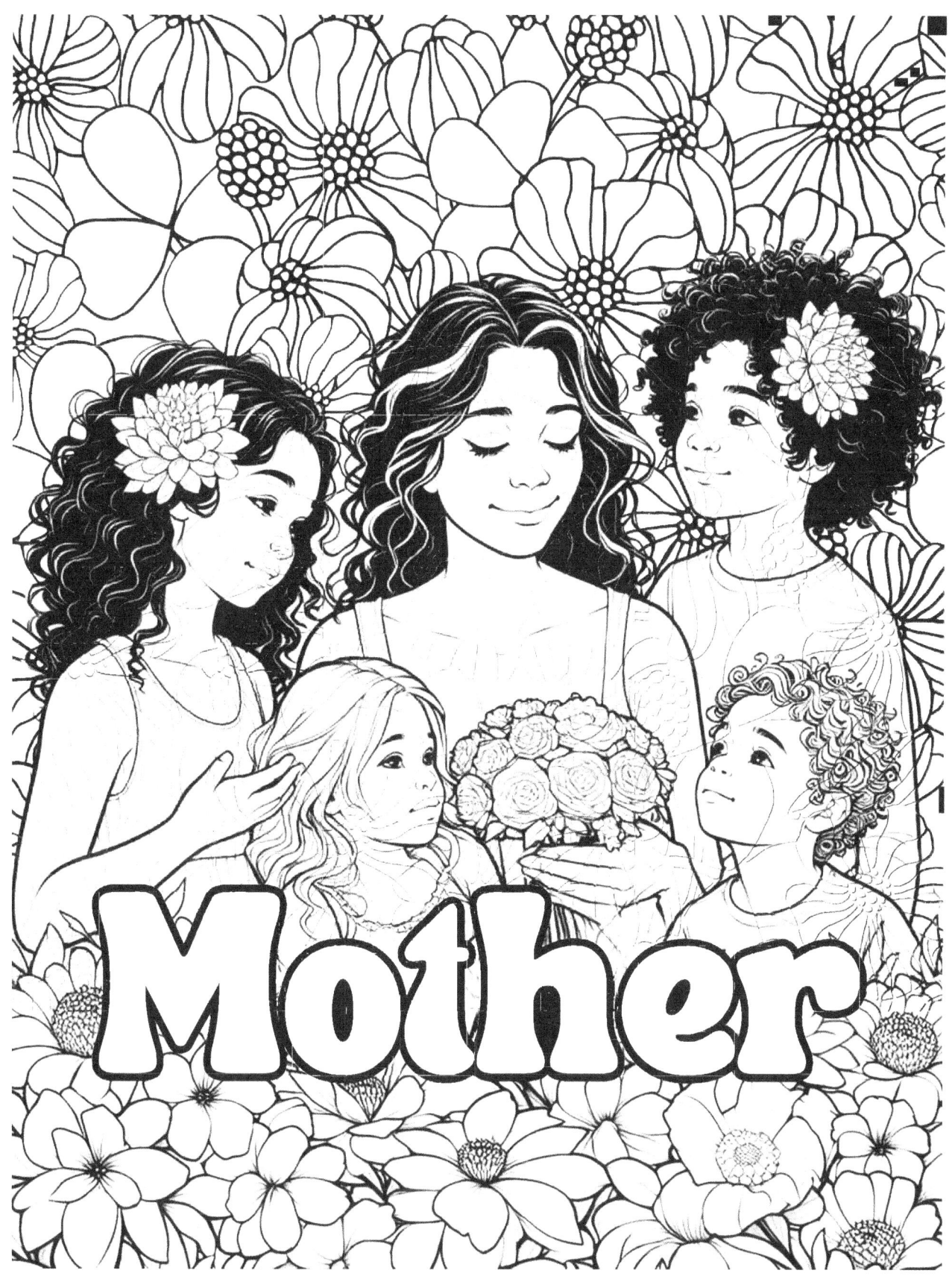

Copyright 2024

All rights reserved.

No portion of this book may be reproduced in any form without written permission from the publisher or author, except as permitted by U.S. copyright law.

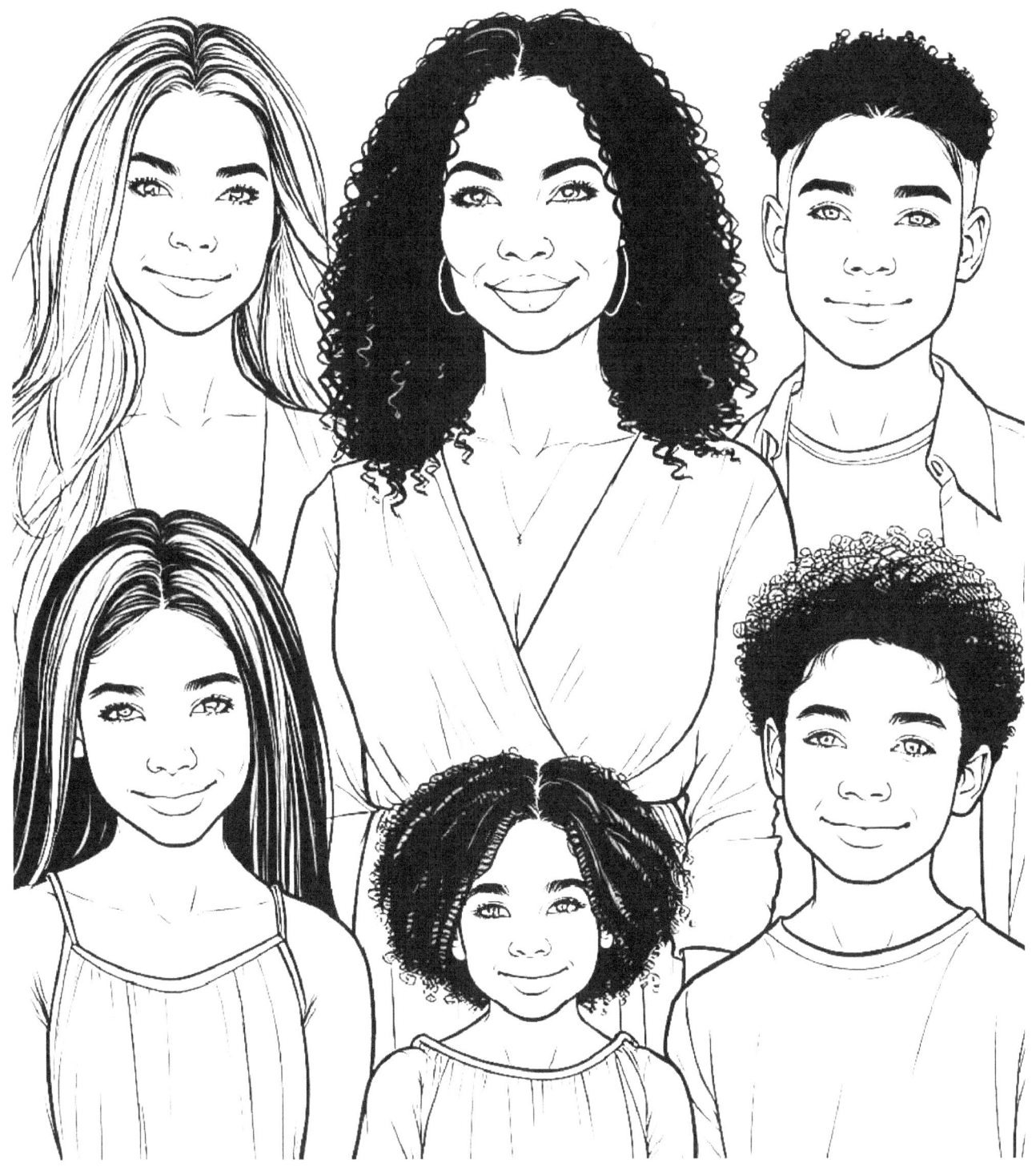

Copyright 2024

All rights reserved.

No portion of this book may be reproduced in any form without written permission from the publisher or author, except as permitted by U.S. copyright law.

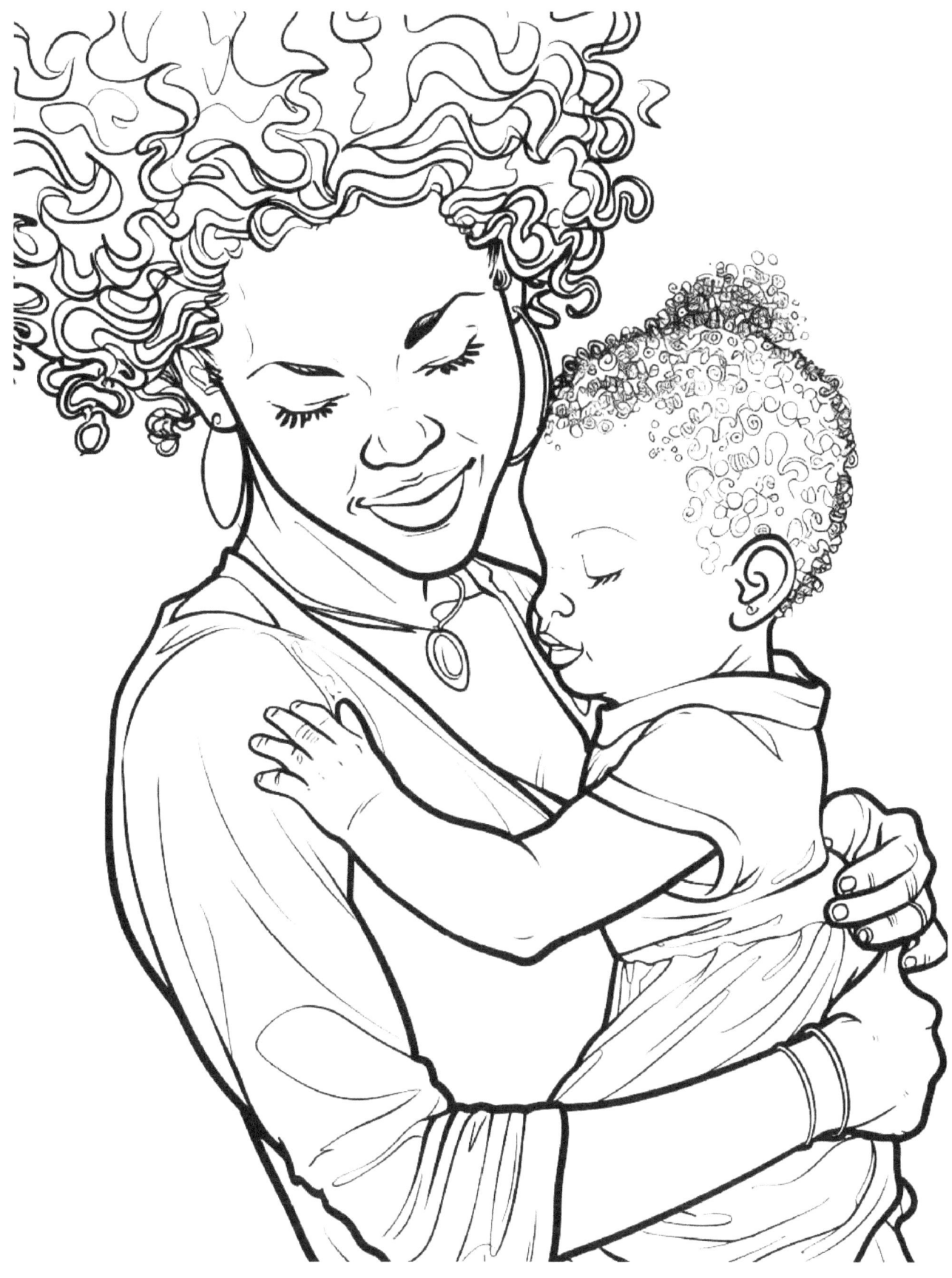

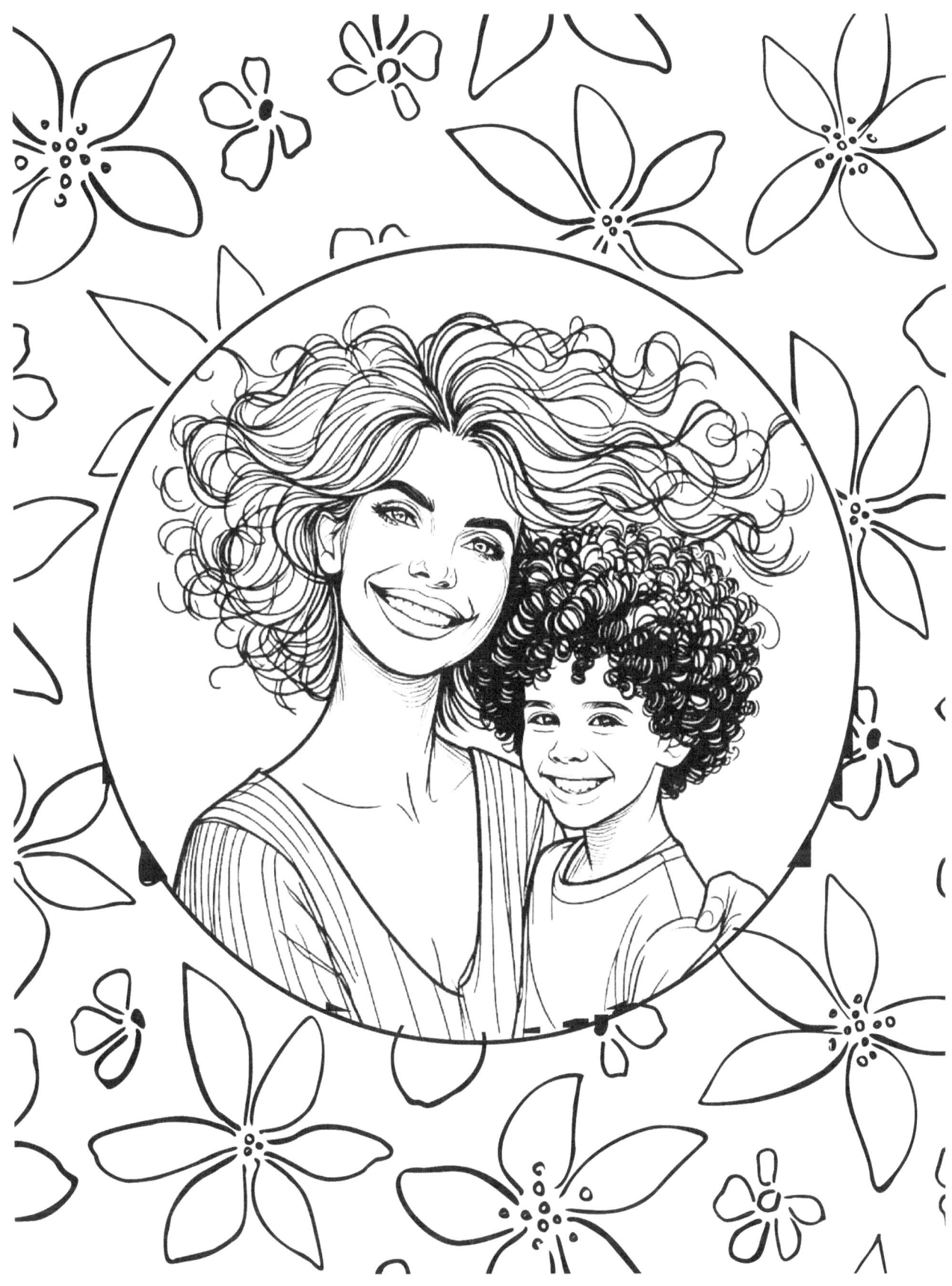

Copyright 2024

All rights reserved.

No portion of this book may be reproduced in any form without written permission from the publisher or author, except as permitted by U.S. copyright law.

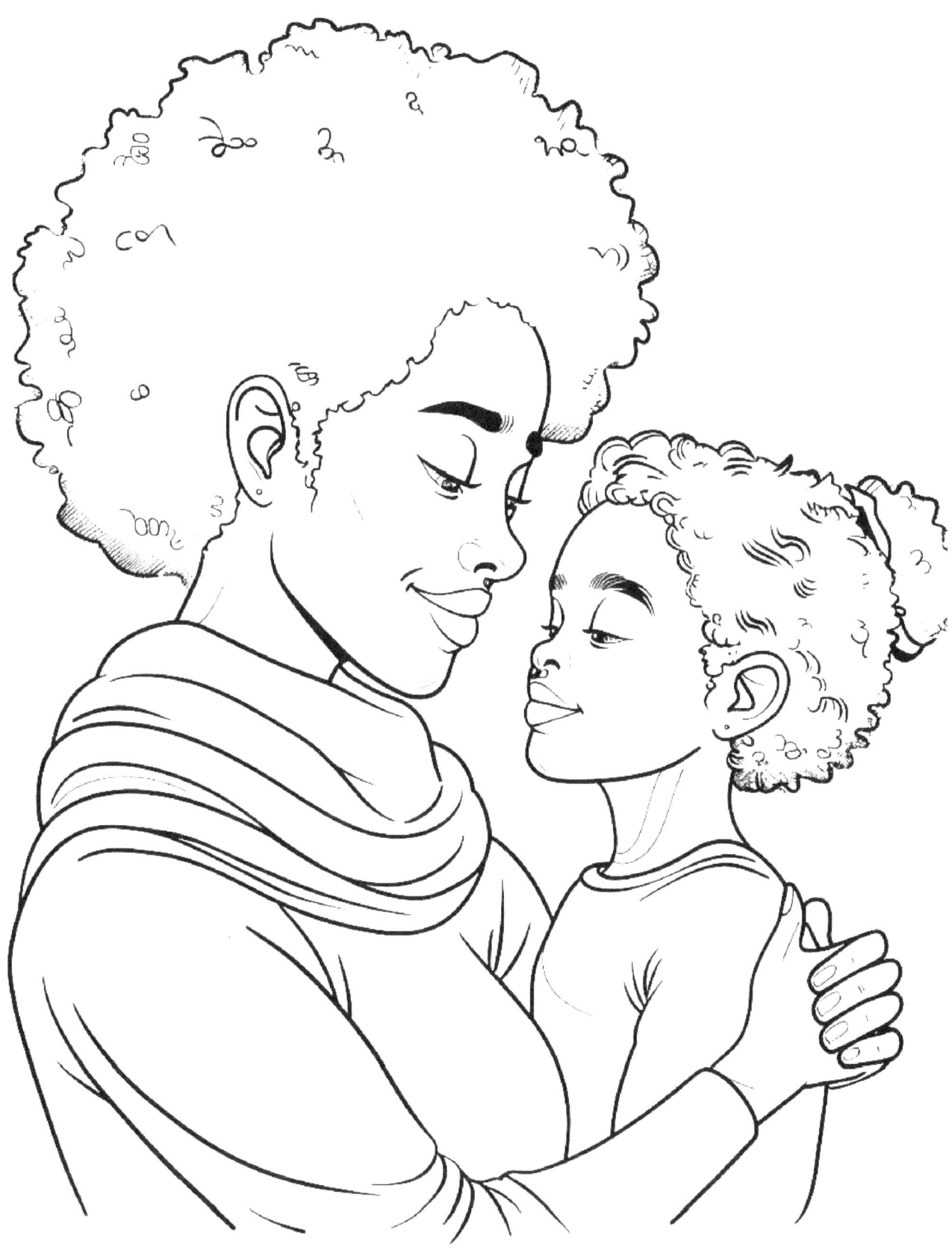

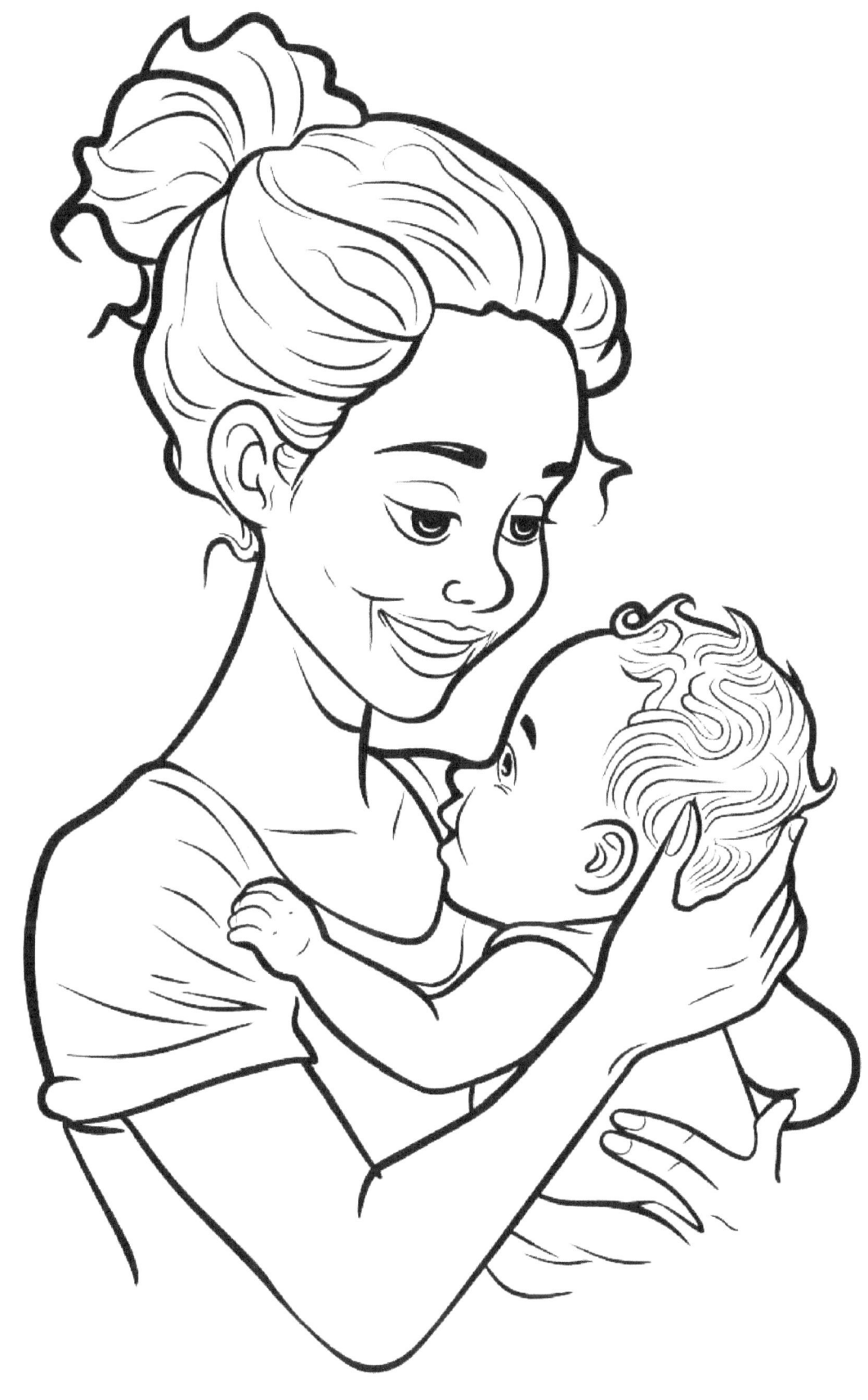

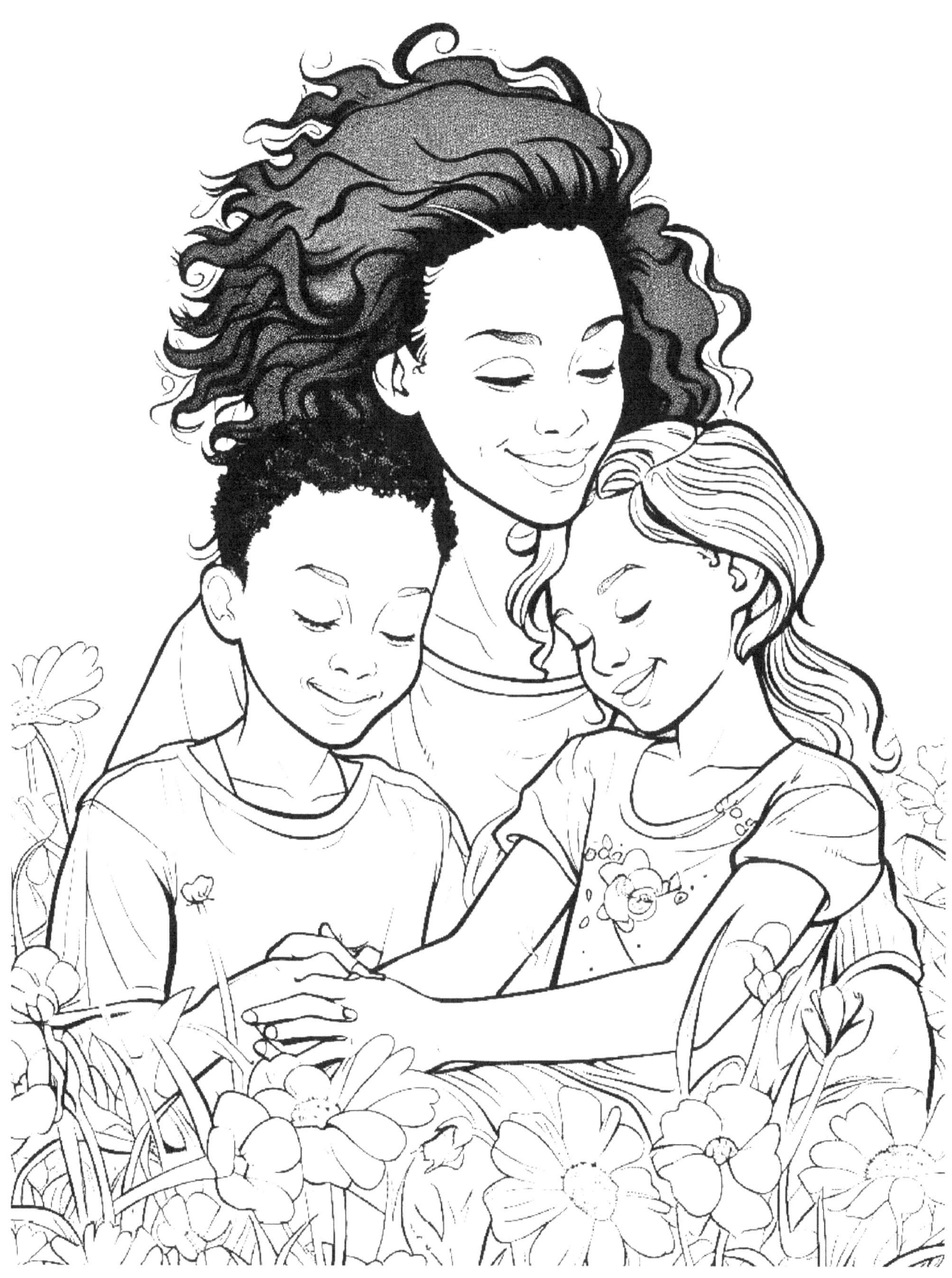

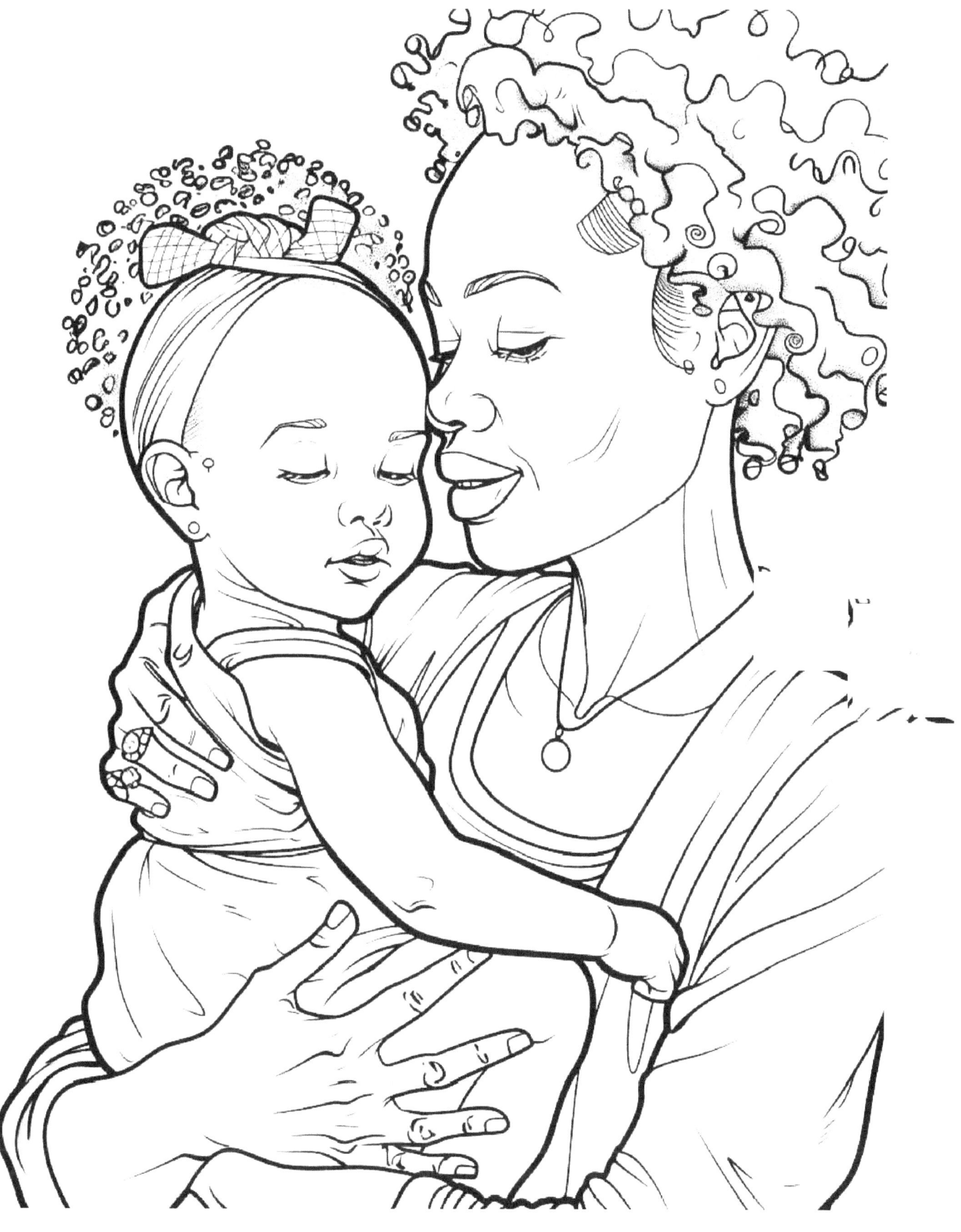

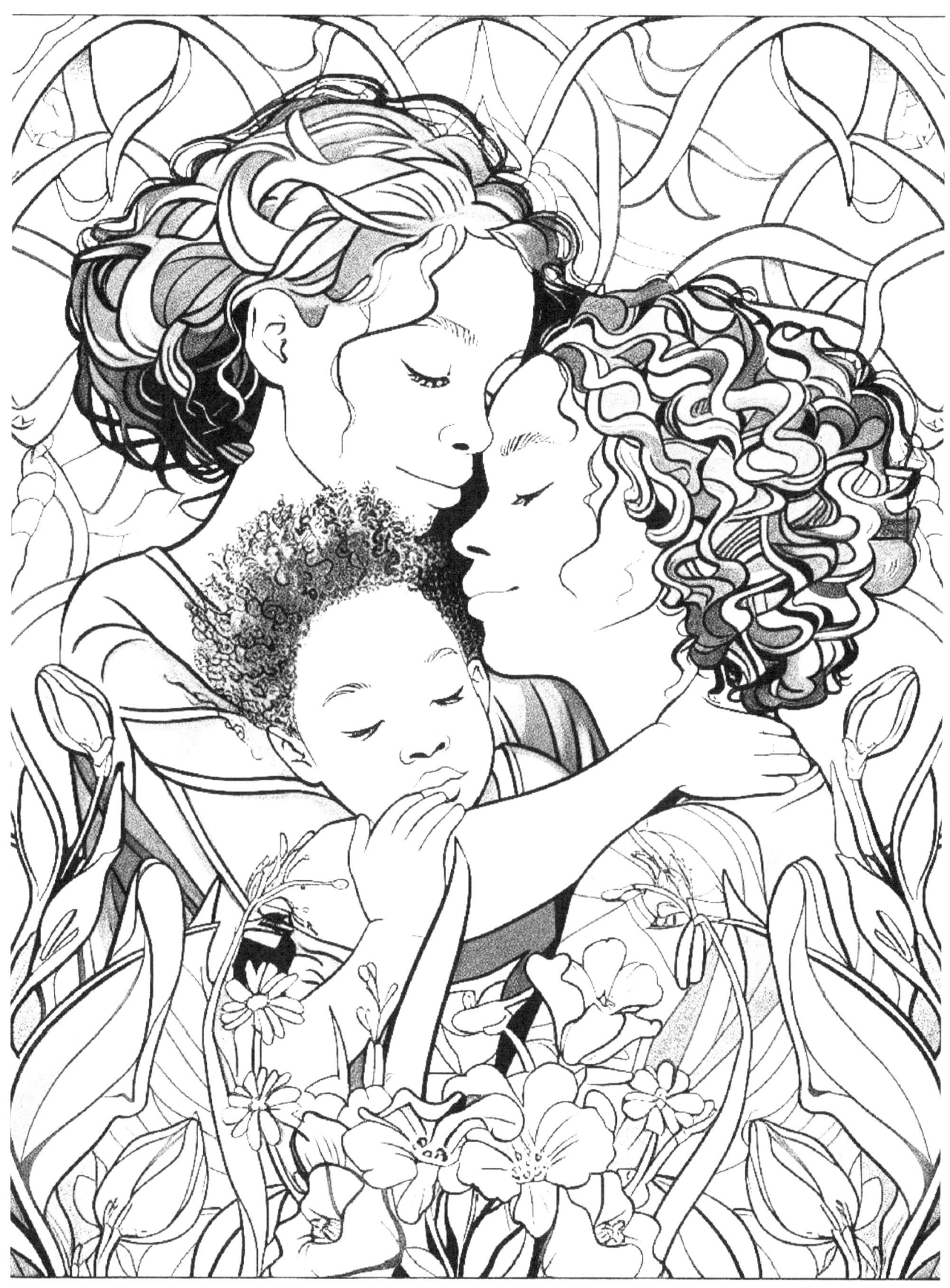

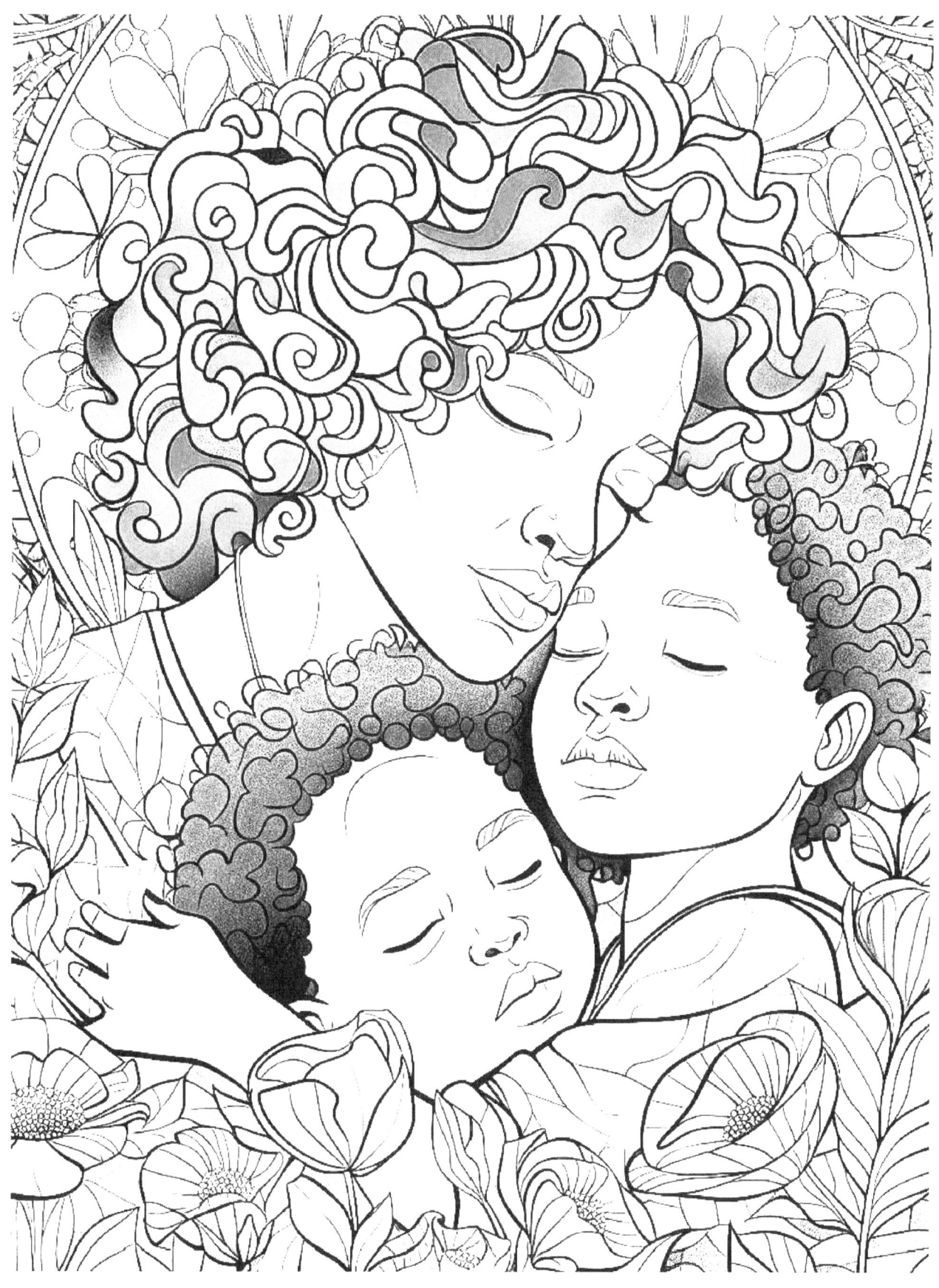

Copyright 2024

All rights reserved.

No portion of this book may be reproduced in any form without written permission from the publisher or author, except as permitted by U.S. copyright law.

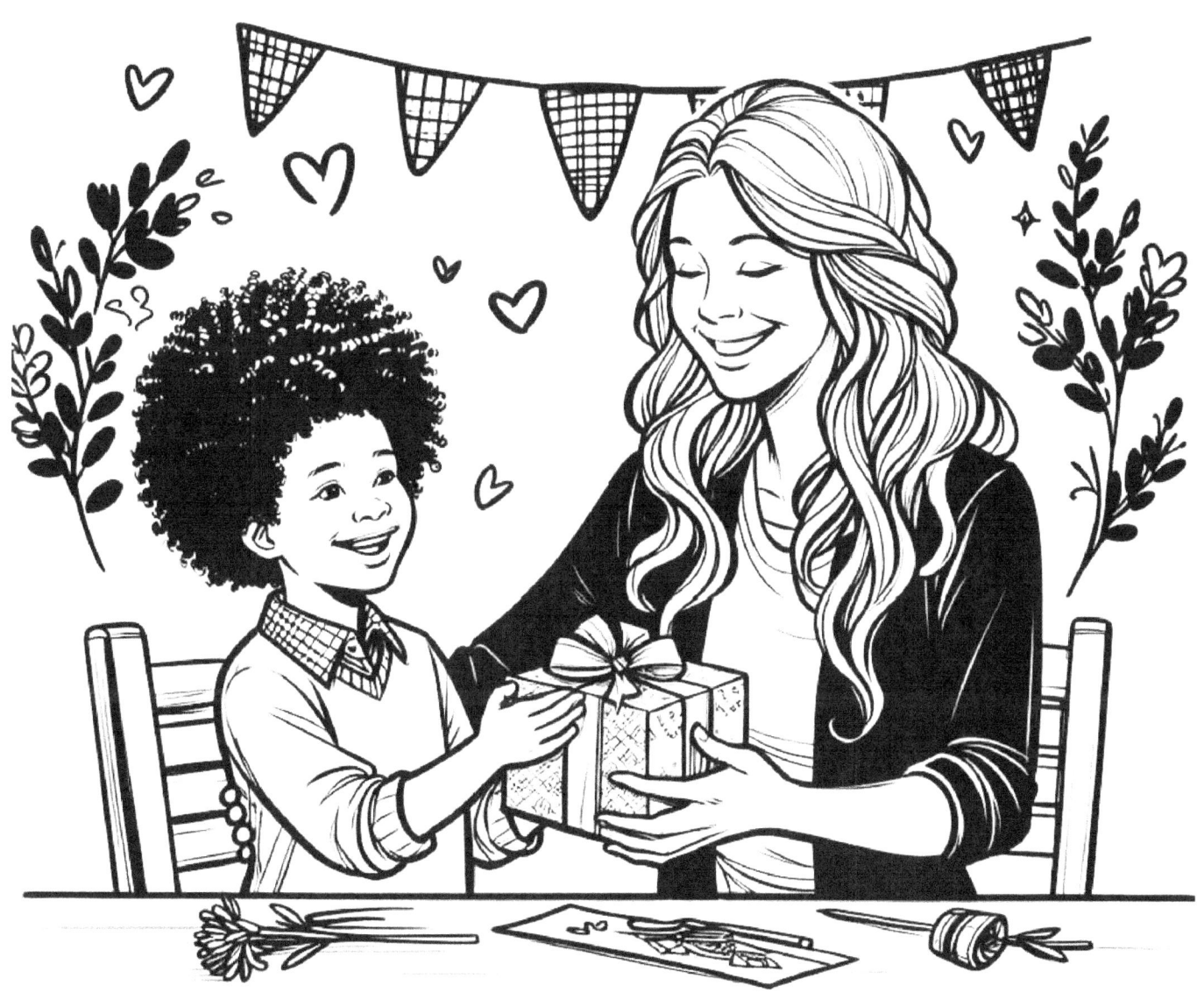

Copyright 2024

All rights reserved.

No portion of this book may be reproduced in any form without written permission from the publisher or author, except as permitted by U.S. copyright law.

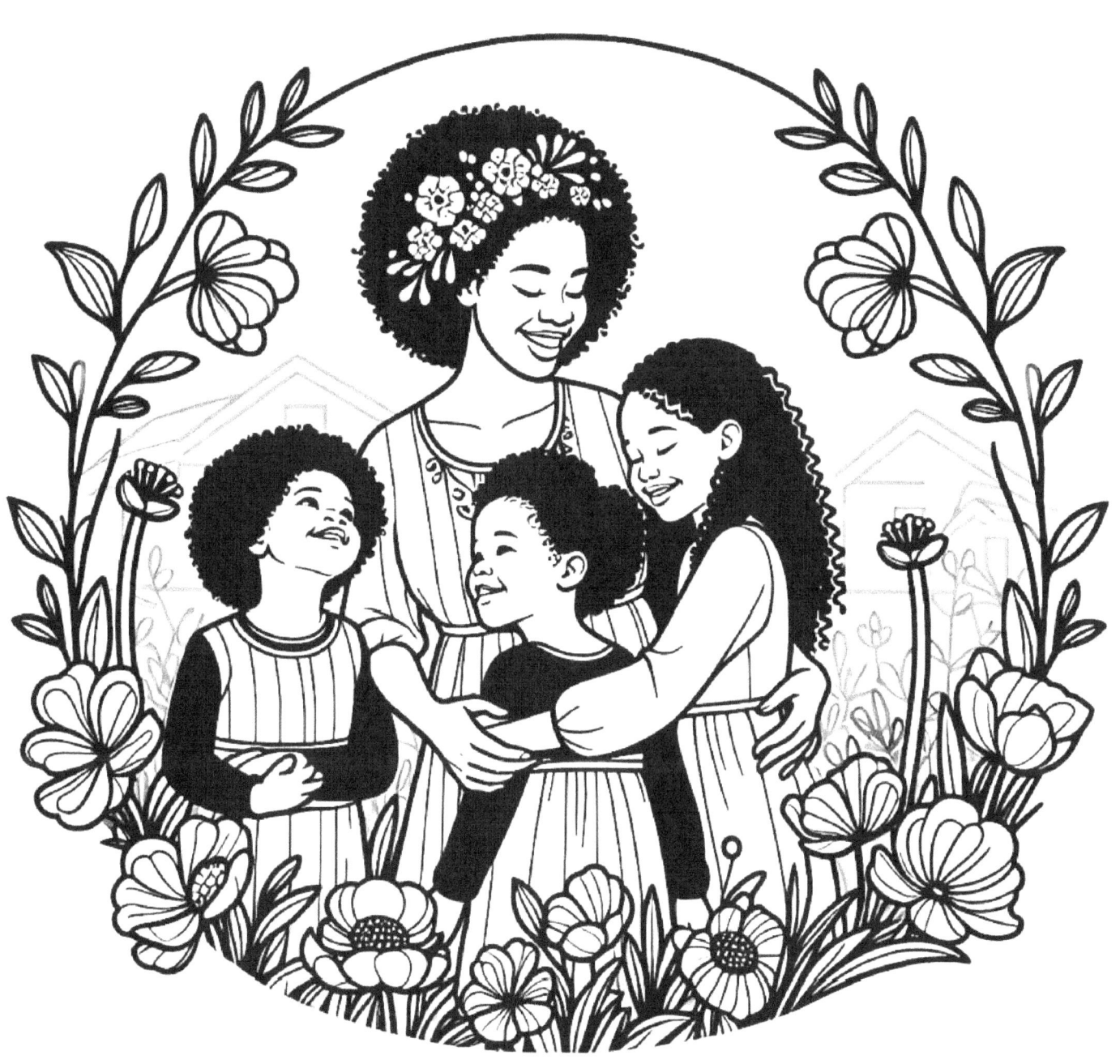

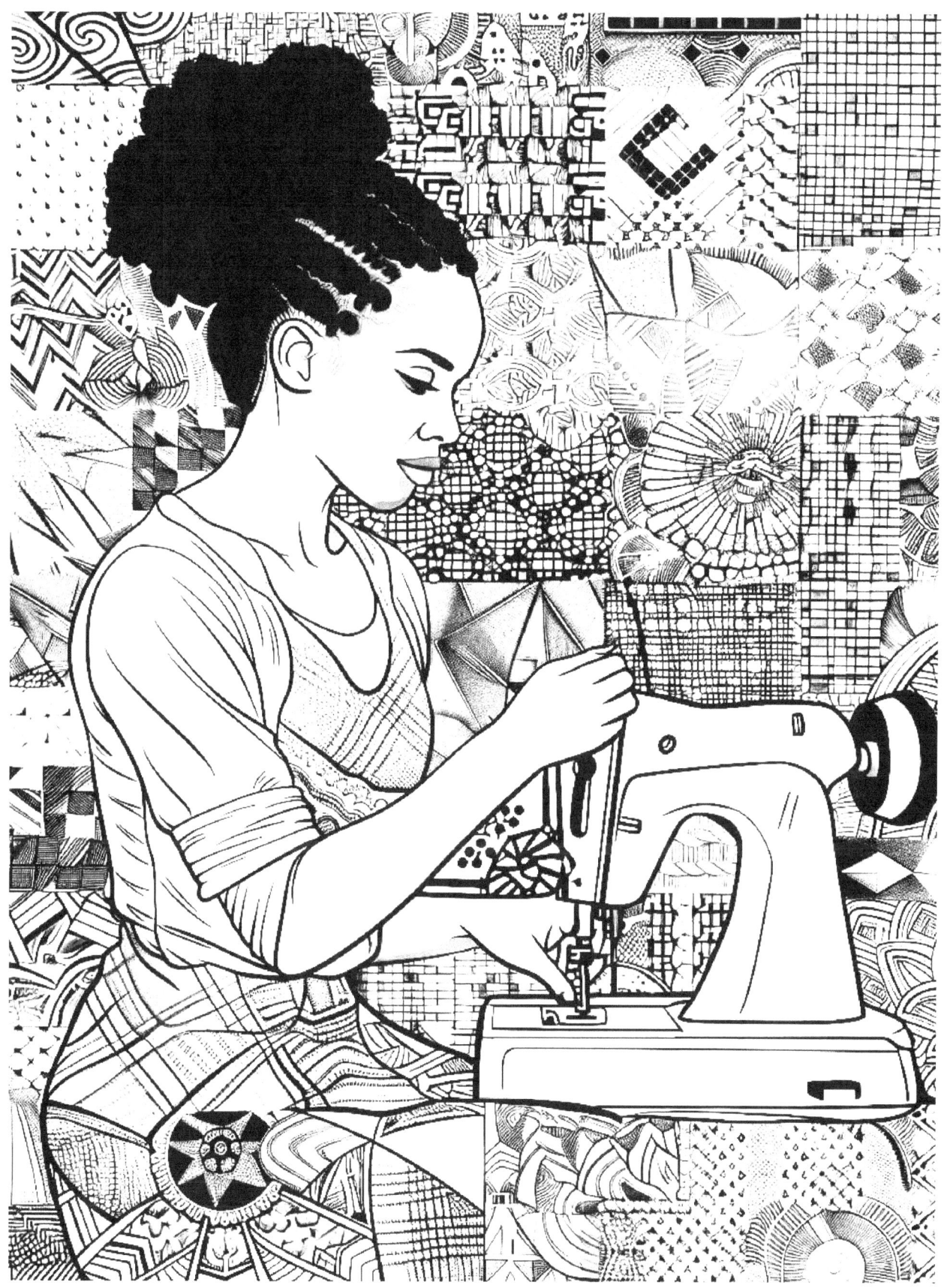

Copyright 2024

All rights reserved.

No portion of this book may be reproduced in any form without written permission from the publisher or author, except as permitted by U.S. copyright law.

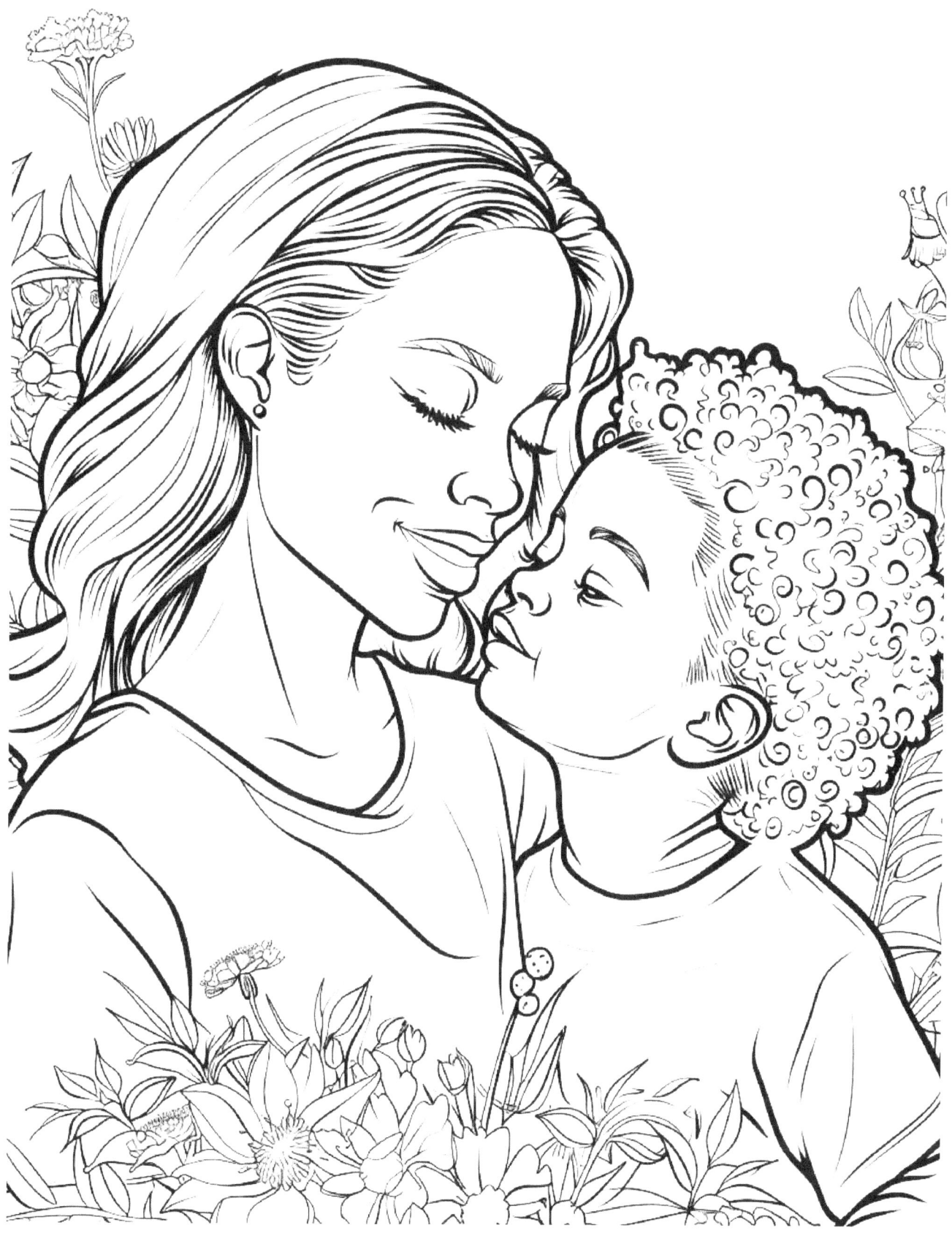

Copyright 2024

All rights reserved.

No portion of this book may be reproduced in any form without written permission from the publisher or author, except as permitted by U.S. copyright law.

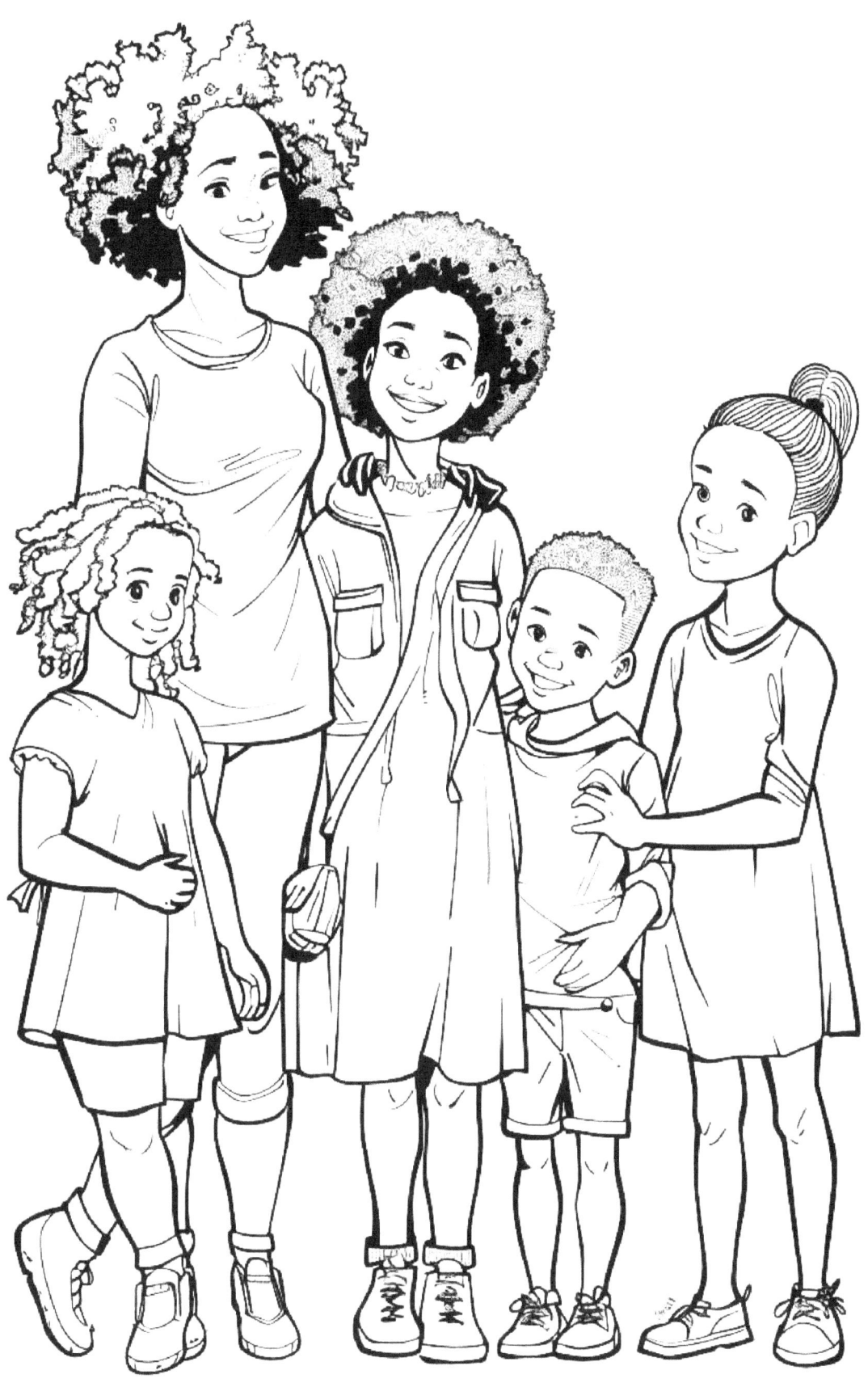

Copyright 2024

All rights reserved.

No portion of this book may be reproduced in any form without written permission from the publisher or author, except as permitted by U.S. copyright law.

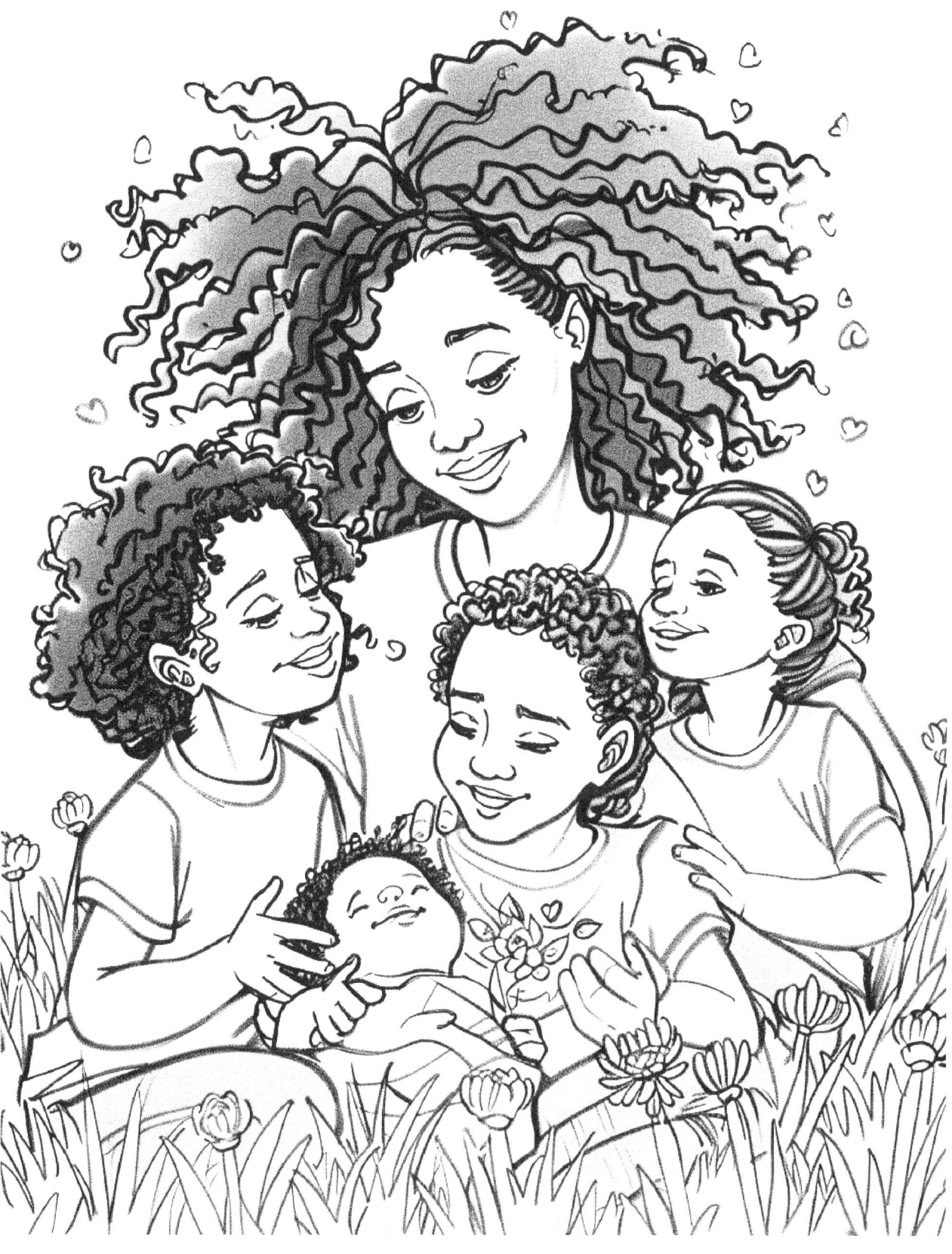

Copyright 2024

All rights reserved.

No portion of this book may be reproduced in any form without written permission from the publisher or author, except as permitted by U.S. copyright law.

MOTHER'S EMBRACE QUOTE'S

"In the embrace of a mother, every color shines brighter; every line tells a story of love."

"Mother's arms: a haven where colors blend, and worries fade."

"Within a mother's embrace, we find the hues of our truest selves."

"A mother's love colors the world with endless warmth and light."

"To be held by a mother is to be woven into a needlepoint of enduring love, each thread a bond that lasts a lifetime."

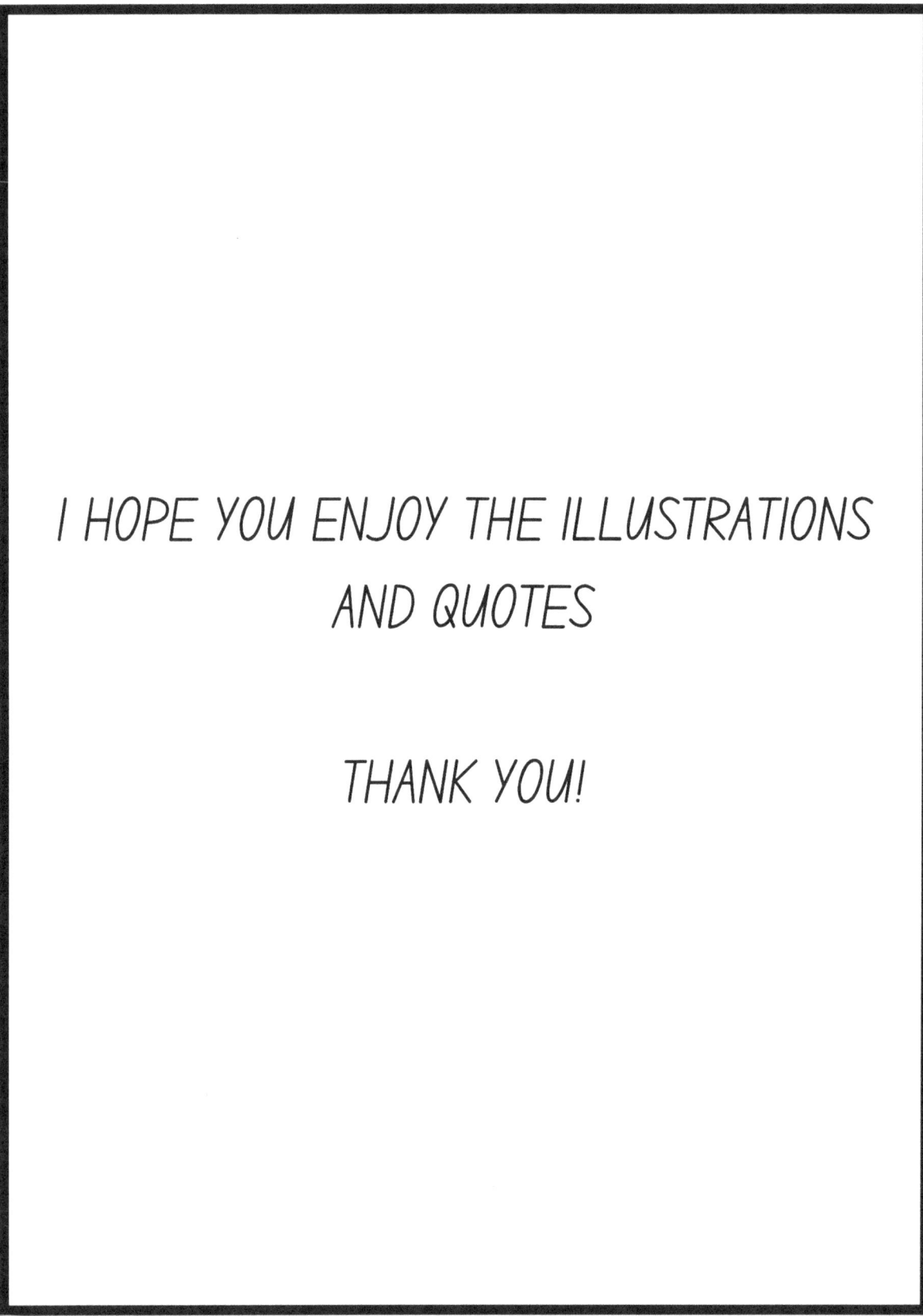

I HOPE YOU ENJOY THE ILLUSTRATIONS AND QUOTES

THANK YOU!